SOUNDS O.K.

TONY WALSH

Folens Publishers

Editor: Deirdre Whelan
Illustrations: Lynn Loftus

© 1996 Folens Limited, on behalf of the author.

First published 1990 by Folens Limited, Dunstable and Dublin.
Folens Limited, Albert House, Apex Business Centre, Boscombe Road, Dunstable, LU5 4RL, England.

Reprinted 1996 and 1997.

ISBN 1 85276 074-5

Printed in Singapore by Craft Print.

Contents

Introduction

The purpose of this book is to continue and extend the work in Phonics and Spelling covered in Teacher Resource Books A, B and C. Generally speaking, children begin school reasonably well advanced in language development.

During the early school years they acquire a basic sight vocabulary. This process continues and soon the children's language development is found to be far ahead of their sight vocabulary.

At this stage it is important that phonic instruction in some form or other be introduced if an acceleration in the children's word recognition skills is to be achieved.

The purpose of this book is to increase the child's knowledge of phonic structure, and thereby to help him or her to a mastery of spelling. It is sufficient to say that without spelling we cannot begin to write.

The spellings to be learned are carefully graded to ensure steady and substantial progress. The carefully selected sentences which may be used as an exercise in dictation provide ample scope for revision and reinforcement of work done.

One might be tempted to begin spelling almost immediately but this step should only be taken when the early phonic work has been sufficiently and thoroughly practised.

It would be impossible to cover all the difficulties found in phonic work but with sufficient practice of the work in this book children should have little difficulty in building and recognising other words within the same phonic families. When reference is made to letter *names* they are written like 'b', 'fr'.

Sounds of letters or groups of letter sounds are written like ⬚ b ⬚ ⬚ fr ⬚ .

The work on consonant sounds in the early part of the book is purely for the benefit of the teacher who will focus the child's attention on the sound associated with each letter.

It should be noted that this book need not be confined to being used in one class only. It may be used with any class the teacher deems appropriate.

Furthermore, *rate of progress* through this book will be at the **complete** discretion of the teacher.

The alphabet

There are 26 letters in the alphabet:

a b c d e f g h i j k l m n o p
q r s t u v w x y z

a e o u i

These are called *vowels.*

The rest of the letters

b c d f g h j k l m n
p q r s t v w x y z

are called *consonants*

    Make sure you know the names of all the letters.

    Most of the letters of the alphabet make different *sounds.*

Consonant sounds

B b	This is one of the first sounds the baby makes. **b - b - b - b** We make that sound when we say **b**at **b**us tu**b**
H h	When we breathe out quickly through our mouths we make this sound. **h - h - h - h** We make that sound at the *start* of these words. **h**at **h**ut **h**ot **h**it
S s	This is the sound the snake makes. **s - s - s - s** We make that sound at the *start* of these words. **s**at **s**it **s**ee

Consonant sounds

M m	When you see something nice which you would like to eat you make the sound this letter makes. **m - m - m - m** We make that sound when we *say* these words **m**ad **m**at Sa**m**
P p	Pretend you are puffing gently at a little feather on the table. You make the sound this letter makes. **p - p - p - p** We make that sound when we say **p**at ca**p** **p**ost
T t	The clock with the pendulum swinging over and back makes this sound **t - t - t - t** We make that sound when we say **t**ap **t**in no**t**

Consonant sounds

G g	When the water in the bath tub is being let out you hear the sound. **g-g-g-g** We make that sound when we say **g**ap **g**et tu**g** 'g' also makes another sound which we will hear about later.
D d	When messages are being sent by morse code the sound this letter makes can be heard. **d-d-d-d** We make that sound at the *start* of these words. **d**a**d** **d**en **d**ip
F f	When my cat gets angry he makes the sound this letter makes. **f-f-f-f** We make that sound at the *start* of these words **f**or **f**ish **f**ast

Consonant sounds

J **j**	This letter says **j - j - j - j** With this letter you can **j**ump and **j**uggle and **j**ingle and **j**angle and **j**og
C **c** **K** **k**	These two letters make the same sound **k - k - k - k** We make that sound when we say the words **c**at **c**ar **k**ite **k**itten sometimes 'C' makes another sound which we will hear about later.
N **n**	"No, no, not nice!". My mum says to my little brother when he picks up something which is dirty. We make that sound too when we say the words ra**n** bar**n** fu**n**

Consonant sounds

Q q	We hear the sound
	
	      q - q- q- q
	
	when we say these words
	
	      quick queen quiz

R r	My dog says
	
	      r - r- r - r
	
	when he runs after a strange cat in our garden.
	We make that sound when we say
	
	      run **r**abbit **r**at

V v	Vincent has the five vowels on his vest. Listen to the **v** sound To make this sound you put your top teeth behind your bottom lip. **v**an **v**ery **v**isit **v**owel Make sure that it is not the **f** sound you say.

L l	With this letter you can
	
	      look, **l**isten and **l**earn.
	
	We make that sound at the *start* of these words
	
	      lion **l**ap **l**ick

Consonant sounds

Y y	When 'y' comes at the beginning of a word it has the same sound as the beginning sound of **y**es, **y**acht and **y**ou. When 'y' comes at the end of a word it can sound like 'e' as in happ**y**, pupp**y**, bab**y**, or it can sound like 'i' as in tr**y**, fl**y**, bu**y**.
W w	I **w**ish I **w**as **w**ith **W**illiam in the **w**ater, Can you hear the w sound? Find other words which have the w sound.
Z z	**z** - **z** - **z** - **z** says the bee as it flies from flower to flower. We make that sound when we say bu**zz** **z**ebra **z**oo.
X x	This letter says **x** as in bo**x** fo**x** si**x**

Vowel sounds

We only use the <u>short</u> sounds of the vowels here - not their names.

a	as in p**a**t, m**a**n b**a**d.
e	as in p**e**t, b**e**d, p**e**g.
o	as in p**o**t, h**o**p, s**o**b.
U	as in p**u**t, m**u**g, r**u**n.
i	as in p**i**t, d**i**g, l**i**p.

Vowels before consonants

a	ab	ad	ag	am
	an	ap	as	at
e	eb	ed	eg	em
	en	ep	et	ex
o	ob	od	og	om
	on	op	ot	ox
u	ub	ud	ug	um
	un	up	ut	us
i	ib	id	ig	im
	in	ip	it	ix

Practise these carefully to make sure you can blend the vowel sound and the consonant sound.

Test yourself like this: (maybe your teacher or your friend will test you)

(i)   What two letters will give the sound ab ? ep ? etc.

(ii) If you blend the letters 'a' and 'b' together what *sound* will you get?

Consonants before vowels

a	ba ca da fa ga ha ja la ma na pa ra sa ta va
e	*be de fe ge *he je le *me ne pe re se te ve *we ye
o	bo co *do fo *go ho jo lo mo *no po ro *so *to
u	bu cu du fu gu hu ju lu mu nu pu ru su tu
i	bi di fi hi ki li mi ni pi ri si ti vi wi

You must have plenty of practice in these builders before going on to the next page. They are called builders because they help us to build many words.

* Note to the teacher:
For the purpose of the word building exercise, these groups of letters should be 'sounded' in the same way as the others in the list.

Word building with the
a builders

By using the **a** builders we can build these words.

A space has been left to make it easy for you to cover the final letter.

Box 1

ba	d
ba	g
ba	n
ba	t

Box 2

ca	b
ca	n
ca	p
ca	t

Box 3

da	b
da	d
da	m
da	n

Box 4

fa	n
fa	t
ga	p
ga	s

Practise the builders carefully again. You can do this by covering the final letter. Then learn the spelling.

Word building with the [a] builders

By using the [a] builders we can build these words.

A space has been left to make it easy for you to cover the final letter

Box 5

ha	d
ha	m
ha	s
ha	t

Box 6

ja	b
ja	m
la	d
la	p

Box 7

ma	d
ma	m
ma	n
ma	t

Box 8

na	b
na	g
na	n
na	p

Practise the builders carefully again. You can do this by covering the final letter. Then learn the spelling.

Word building with the [a] builders

By using the [a] builders we can build these words.

A space has been left to make it easy for you to cover the final letter

Box 9

pa	d
pa	l
pa	n
pa	t

Box 10

ra	g
ra	n
ra	p
ra	t

Box 11

sa	d
sa	g
Sa	m
sa	t

Box 12

ta	g
ta	n
ta	p
va	n

Practise the builders carefully again. You can do this by covering the final letter. Then learn the spelling.

Time for a test

1. Dad had a mat in the cab.

2. The bad cat had the ham.

3. Pat ran to the van.

4. Fat Dan had a cap.

5. Sam sat at the dam.

6. Mam has a rag at the tap.

7. The fat cat had a nap on the mat.

8. I had jam in the can.

9. The cat has the rat.

10. The man has a fan in the van.

Word building with the e builders

By using the e builders we can build these words.

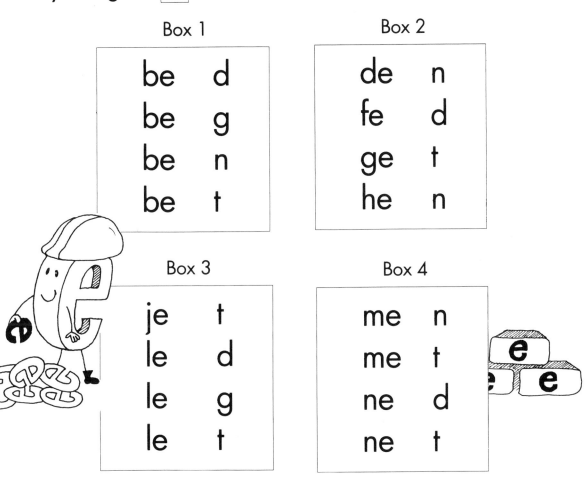

Box 1

be	d
be	g
be	n
be	t

Box 2

de	n
fe	d
ge	t
he	n

Box 3

je	t
le	d
le	g
le	t

Box 4

me	n
me	t
ne	d
ne	t

Cover the final letter with a book and practise the builders first of all. Then add the final sound.
Learn to spell the words.

Word building with the $\boxed{e}$ builders

By using the $\boxed{e}$ builders we can build these words.

Box 5		Box 6		Box 7	
re	d	pe	g	ve	t
Re	x	pe	n	we	t
se	t	pe	t	we	b
te	n	pe	p	ye	t
Te	d			ye	s

Cover the final letter with a book and practise the builders first of all. Then add the final sound. Learn to spell the words.

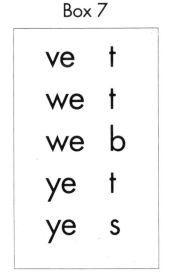
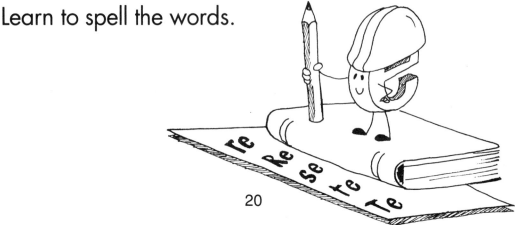

20

Time for a test

1. Ned met Peg at the den.

2. Rex has the leg of ham.

3. Ben has a red pen set.

4. The men had a net in the bag.

5. I can get Ted at ten.

6. Dan had ten fat hens.

7. I met Sam at the jet.

8. Mam fed the hens.

9. Let Ben get the bat.

10. Rex sat on the wet bed.

Word building with the **o** builders

The **o** builders help us to build these words.

Box 1			Box 2		
bo	b		co	d	
bo	g		co	g	
bo	p		co	p	
bo	x		co	t	

Box 3			Box 4		
do	g		Go	d	
do	t		go	t	
fo	g		jo	b	
fo	x		jo	g	

Practise the builders carefully.
Make sure you know the word.
Learn to spell the word.

22

Word building with the o builders

The o builders help us to build these words.

Box 5

ho	b
ho	g
ho	p
ho	t

Box 6

lo	b
lo	g
lo	p
lo	t

Box 7

mo	b
mo	p
no	d
no	t

Box 8

so	b
so	d
To	m
to	p

Practise the builders carefully.
Make sure you know the word.
Learn to spell the word.

Word building with the 🅾 builders

The 🅾 builders help us to build these words.

Box 9		Box 10	
po	d	ro	b
po	p	ro	d
po	t	ro	t

Practise the builders carefully.
Make sure you know the word.
Learn to spell the word.

Time for a test

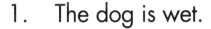

1. The dog is wet.

2. Tom has the box in the pot.

3. The cat is not in the cot.

4. The man got a cod on the rod.

5. The red fox ran to the bog.

6. Sam has got a job.

7. The mad mob got Ted in the fog.

8. I can hop on the wet logs.

9. Peg had the pot on the hot hob.

10. Hop to the log box.

Word building with the $\boxed{u}$ builders

The $\boxed{u}$ builders help us to build these words.

Box 1

bu	d
bu	g
bu	n
bu	t

Box 2

du	b
du	g
fu	n

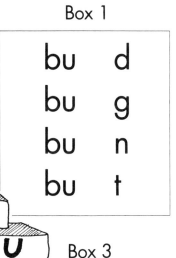

Box 3

gu	m
gu	n
nu	n
nu	t

Box 4

su	m
su	n
tu	b
tu	g

Practise the builders carefully.
Make sure you know the word.
Learn to spell the word.

Word building with the
u builders

The **u** builders help us to build these words.

Box 5

pu	p
pu	t
ru	b
ru	g

Box 6

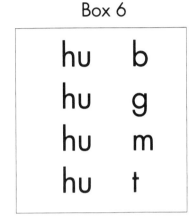

hu	b
hu	g
hu	m
hu	t

Box 7

cu	b
cu	p
cu	t

Box 8

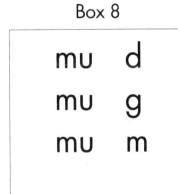

mu	d
mu	g
mu	m

Practise the builders carefully.
Make sure you know the word.
Learn to spell the word.

Time for a test

1. The fox cub ran to the hut.

2. The men dug in the bog.

3. I put the mug on the cup.

4. Tom got the tub for mum.

5. The pups and the cats are fed.

6. Do not rub the wet rug.

7. I cannot put the bud in the pot.

8. Pat had fun but cut his leg.

9. Mum got a big hug.

10. Sam led the men and got the cup.

Word building with the
i builders

The **i** builders help us to build these words.

Box 1

bi	b
bi	d
bi	g
bi	n
bi	t

Box 2

di	g
di	d
di	n
di	m
di	p

Box 3

hi	d
hi	m
hi	p
hi	s
hi	t

Box 4

fi	g
fi	n
fi	t
fi	x
mi	x

Practise the builders carefully.
Make sure you know the word.
Learn to spell the word.

Word building with the
i builders

The **i** builders help us to build these words.

Box 5

Ji	m
Ki	m
ni	b
ni	p

Box 6

pi	g
pi	n
pi	t
pi	p

Box 7

si	n
si	p
si	t
si	x

Box 8

ri	b
ri	p
wi	g
wi	n

Box 9

Ti	m
ti	n
ti	p

Practise the builders carefully.
Make sure you know the word.
Learn to spell the word.

Time for a test

1. Did Jim sit on top of the bin?

2. Mum hid the guns in the red hut.

3. Sam got a big pig and a dog.

4. I sat on the pin.

5. Did Kim hit Pat in the ribs?

6. Mum rips the rags.

7. Jim put the lid on the log box.

8. Dan has a box of buns.

9. Tim had to sit in the wet pit.

10. Did Dan fix the cot for mum?

Magic

Magic **e** or silent **e** gives **a** its own name.
The long vowel sound is marked like this **ā**.

Box 1		Box 2	
can	cān**e**	hat	hāt**e**
pan	pān**e**	mat	māt**e**
dan	dān**e**	rat	rāt**e**

Box 3		Box 4	
dam	dām**e**	gap	gāp**e**
sam	sām**e**	mad	mād**e**
fad	fād**e**	pal	pāl**e**

Other words ending in silent **e**.

Box 5	Box 6	Box 7
āp**e**	cāk**e**	cās**e**
dāt**e**	rāk**e**	nām**e**
gāt**e**	sāk**e**	mān**e**
lāt**e**	tāk**e**	lān**e**

The **e** keeps quiet.

Time for a test

1. Dad has a *cap* but Mum has a *cape*.

2. *Can* Tom get the big *cane*?

3. Kim has a red *hat* but I *hate* it.

4. Get the *mat* for your *mate*.

5. We cannot get the *rat* at this *rate*.

6. *Sam* has the *same* bat as you.

7. The hot *tap* has no *tape* on it.

8. My *pal* is in bed and he is *pale*.

9. My Dad was *mad* with the din the jet *made*.

Magic e

Magic **e** or silent **e** gives **o** its own name.
The long vowel sound is marked like this **ō**.

Box 1	Box 2

	Box 1		Box 2
cod	cōde	cop	cōpe
rod	rōde	hop	hōpe
rob	rōbe	pop	pōpe

Other words ending in silent **e**

Box 3

rōse
hōse
nōse
dōze

Box 4

hōle
sōle
pōle
mōle

Box 5

wōre
cōre
sōre
tōre

Box 6

jōke
cōke
pōke
woke

Box 7

cōne
bōne
tōne
home

The **e** keeps quiet.

Time for a test

1. If you *hop* I *hope* you do not get wet.

2. Do *not* cut the *note*.

3. *Rob* has a red *robe*.

4. The dog got the *rod* as I *rode*.

5. *Con* had a big *cone*.

6. There is a *hole* in my shoe.

7. The *bone* in my *nose* is *sore*.

8. Pat put the *pole* in the big *hole*.

9. The *Pope* is in *Rome*.

10. *Rose tore* the red rag.

Magic

Magic **e** or silent **e** gives **u** its own name.
The long vowel is marked like this **ū**.

	Box 1
cub	cūbe
cut	cūte
tub	tūbe
us	ūse

Other words ending in silent **e**.

Box 2	Box 3	Box 4
fūse	cūre	rūle
Lūke	sūre	mūle
tūne	pūre	rūde
Jūne	mūte	nūde

The **e** keeps quiet.
1. The *cub* is in the *cube*.
2. Mum *cut* the hair of the *cute* pup.
3. The *tub* has a *tube* in it.

Magic e

Magic **e** or silent **e** gives **i** its own name.
The long vowel sound is marked like this **ī**.

	Box 1			Box 2
bit	bīt**e**	hid		hīd**e**
dim	dīm**e**	pin		pīn**e**
din	dīn**e**	pip		pīp**e**
fin	fīn**e**	rip		rīp**e**
wīn	wīn**e**	Tim		tīm**e**

Other words ending in silent **e**

Box 3	Box 4	Box 5
fīl**e**	rīd**e**	līk**e**
pīl**e**	tīd**e**	hīk**e**
mīl**e**	wīd**e**	bīk**e**
tīl**e**	sīd**e**	pīk**e**

Box 6	Box 7	Box 8
fīv**e**	fīr**e**	wīf**e**
dīv**e**	hīr**e**	līf**e**
hīv**e**	wīr**e**	wīs**e**
alīv**e**	mīr**e**	sīz**e**

The **e** keeps quiet.

Time for a test

1. Tom put the *pip* into the *pipe*.

2. Give Rex a *bit* and he will *bite* it.

3. It was *dim* and he had not got a *dime*.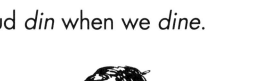

4. Dad will *win* the *wine*.

5. *Tim* said it was *time* to go.

6. The *pin* fell into the *pine* tree.

7. Pat *hid* the box but Peg could not *hide* it.

8. Do not *rip* your dress getting the *ripe* apples.

9. This *fin* is a *fine* one.

10. My family make a loud *din* when we *dine*.

Useful words

Box 1

why
who
when
where
what

Box 2

was
were
have
has
had

Box 3

he
she
you
we
our

Box 4

school
house
play
work
field

Box 5

mother
father
grandmother
grandfather

Box 6

uncle
aunt
brother
sister

Box 7

boy
girl
baby
friend

Box 8

said
saw
they
them

Useful words

Box 1

head
eye
nose
ear

Box 2

mouth
nose
tongue
finger

Box 3

on
off
came
went

Box 4

days
Monday
Tuesday
Wednesday

Box 5

Thursday
Friday
Saturday
Sunday

Box 6

January
February
March
April

Box 7

May
June
July
August

Box 8

September
October
November
December

s + h = sh

These two letters together make one sound.

sh

sh - sh - sh
The baby is asleep!

Practise these builders before trying the words.

sha	***she**	**sho**	**shu**	**shi**
Box 1	Box 2	Box 3	Box 4	Box 5
shall	shed	shop	shut	ship
sham	shell	shot	shun	shin
shame	Shep	shore	shunt	shine

Don't forget what silent **e** does in the words underlined.

sh at the end of a word

Box 6	ash	dash	mash	wash
Box 7	hush	bush	push	mesh
Box 8	fish	wish	dish	posh

Note to Teacher: For the purpose of the exercise this word should be sounded phonetically.

41

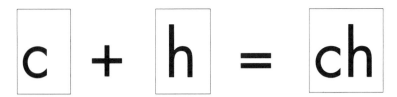

These two letters together make one sound.

ch - ch - ch the train
says as it chugs along the track.

Practise these builders.

cha   che   cho   chu   chi

box 1 | chap   chess   chop   chum   chip

ch at the end of a word

Box 2	Box 3	Box 4
batch	bench	bunch
hatch	notch	hitch
patch	such	witch
catch	much	church

Sometimes **ch** has the sound of **k**

Box 5 | Christ   Christmas   chemist   school

Can you find any other word where
ch has a **k** sound?

42

Time for a test

1. The child went into the shed.

2. Did your dad chop down the big bush?

3. I shall get shells on the shore.

4. I eat fish and chips in the chip shop.

5. Push the latch on the hatch.

6. I wish I could play chess.

7. Pat saw a bunch of keys at the church gate.

8. Shep will catch the cat in the wide patch.

9. The witch has a big nose.

10. I did not wash the red rash on my chin.

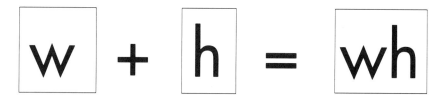

These two letters together make one sound.

 Listen to the **wh** sound in these words.

what   **wh**ere   **wh**en   **wh**y

Practise the **wha whe whi** builders.

Box 1

what
when
where
whale

Box 2

whip
whistle
which
whisper

When **wh** is followed by **o** sometimes it has a **h** sound as in these two words:

who   whole

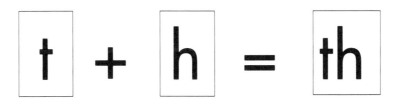

These two letters together make one sound.

The letters **th** make the sound **th** as in

Box 1

| three | thin | think | thank | thumb |

or

they make a different sound as in

Box 2

| then | this | father | mother |

Box 3

| that |
| than |
| there |
| them |

Box 4

| cloth |
| moth |
| broth |
| mouth |

Box 5

| tooth |
| teeth |
| bath |
| with |

Box 6

| thirty |
| thorn |
| Thursday |
| thump |

Box 7 | throb | thread | thrush | fifth |

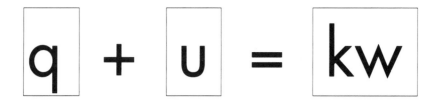

q + u = kw

These two letters together make one sound.

u always follows **q**.

Together they make the sound **kw** .

Listen to the sound as you say

Box 1

quite

queen

quiet

Box 2

quiz

question

quilt

qu always has another vowel right after the **u**.

46

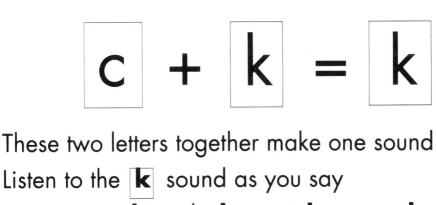

c + k = k

These two letters together make one sound **k**

Listen to the **k** sound as you say

pack   luck   sick   peck

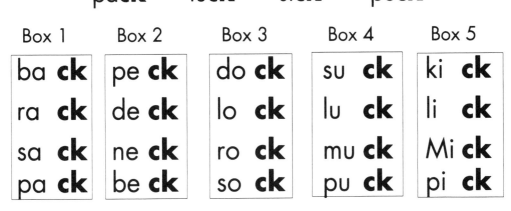

Box 1	Box 2	Box 3	Box 4	Box 5
ba **ck**	pe **ck**	do **ck**	su **ck**	ki **ck**
ra **ck**	de **ck**	lo **ck**	lu **ck**	li **ck**
sa **ck**	ne **ck**	ro **ck**	mu **ck**	Mi **ck**
pa **ck**	be **ck**	so **ck**	pu **ck**	pi **ck**

Practise the builders first of all by covering the **ck**.

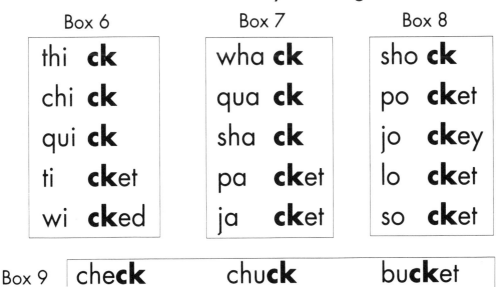

Box 6	Box 7	Box 8
thi **ck**	wha **ck**	sho **ck**
chi **ck**	qua **ck**	po **ck**et
qui **ck**	sha **ck**	jo **ck**ey
ti **ck**et	pa **ck**et	lo **ck**et
wi **ck**ed	ja **ck**et	so **ck**et

Box 9 | che**ck**   chu**ck**   bu**ck**et |

No word ever starts with **ck**.

Time for a test

1. Put the lock in your back pocket.

2. The chick cannot say quack.

3. This ticket was stuck to the white packet.

4. Where did the jockey get the muck on his jacket?

5. My brother has all the quiz questions.

6. Why did you whistle at Dick?

7. On Thursday the queen had a quiet chat with Mick.

8. There are thirty days in each of four months.

9. When did you get the thick thorn in your thumb?

10. Do you think my teeth are white?

a, e, o, u, i followed by 'r'

When a vowel is followed by **r** the sound of the vowel may be slightly changed

ar	as in c**ar**, f**ar**, **ar**m
er	as in aft**er**, f**er**n, summ**er**
or	as in f**or**, b**or**n, act**or**
ur	as in f**ur**, b**ur**n, ch**ur**n
ir	as in b**ir**d, wh**ir**l, f**ir**m

ar   er   or   ur   ir

Box 1	Box 9	Box 17	Box 25	Box 33
far	fern	for	fur	sir
tar	herd	fork	turn	bird
bar	shepherd	cork	burn	third

Box 2	Box 10	Box 18	Box 26	Box 34
card	herald	born	churn	first
hard	hermit	corn	church	dirt
lard	heron	horn	hurt	girl

Box 3	Box 11	Box 19	Box 27	Box 35
cart	after	form	purse	whirl
dart	dinner	horse	nurse	shirt
part	winter	north	curse	birch

Box 4	Box 12	Box 20	Box 28	Box 36
tart	summer	short	curl	thirsty
mart	better	sort	hurt	dirty
chart	letter	lord	turf	birthday

ar　　er　　or　　ur

Box 5
bark
dark
park

Box 13
teacher
father
mother

Box 21
actor
visitor
doctor

Box 29
purple
urgent
turkey

Box 6
lark
mark
shark

Box 14
sister
other
brother

Box 22
error
tractor
motor

Box 30
turnip
return
Saturday

Box 7
harm
farm
charm

Box 15
better
older
bigger

Box 23
morning
forget
torch

Box 31
burden
surface
murmur

Box 8
sharp
garden
carpet

Box 16
longer
shorter
softer

Box 24
orange
forty
forest

Box 32
further
purchase
surprise

Time for a test

1. The nurse led my brother into the doctor when he was sick.

2. I stay in bed every Saturday morning in winter.

3. My older brother is much bigger than my sister.

4. The actor was born forty years ago.

5. My shirt was dirty when I fell in the garden.

6. Get a bigger turnip for the dinner.

7. Where did the teacher get the purple and orange jacket?

8. The horse fell and the jockey was hurt on the hard surface.

9. Some birds have longer legs than others.

10. The hermit had a sharp thorn in his finger.

br   cr

br	Practise the consonants **b** and **r** separately before blending them. Think of as many words as you can that begin with **br** .

Then practise the builders.

bra	**bre**	**bro**	**bru**	**bri**
Box 1	Box 2	Box 3	Box 4	Box 5
brat	bred	bronze	brush	brim
brag	Brendan	broth	brunch	brick
brass	br**ee**ze	broke	brute	bride

ee together make the long vowel sound $\bar{e}$.

cr	Practise the consonants **c** and **r** separately before blending them. (**cr** sounds as **kr**) Think of as many words as you can that begin with **cr**.

Then practise the builders

cra	**cre**	**cro**	**cru**	**cri**
Box 6	Box 7	Box 8	Box 9	Box 10
crab	crest	crop	crust	crib
cram	cress	cross	crush	cricket
crash	crept	crock	crude	crime

Two consonants which are the same, sound as only one
– bra**ss** cre**ss** cro**ss**

Practise the consonants **d** and **r** separately before blending them.
Think of as many words as you can that begin with **dr** .

Then practise the builders.

dra	**dre**	**dro**	**dru**	**dri**
Box 1	Box 2	Box 3	Box 4	Box 5
drag	dregs	drop	drug	drip
dram	dress	drove	drum	drill
drape	dresser	drone	drub	drive

 Practise the consonants **f** and **r** separately before blending them.
Think of as many words as you can that begin with **fr** .

Then practise the builders

fra	**fre**	**fro**	**fri**
Box 6	Box 7	Box 8	Box 9
Frank	Fred	frog	frill
frame	fresh	frock	fritter
frantic	freckles	frost	

Do you remember what **e** does in these words?

drap**e**   drov**e**   driv**e**   fram**e**

Time for a test

1.   Brendan broke the drill on the brick wall.

2.   The bride had a nice frill on her white dress.

3.   Did the driver crash the car on the frost on Friday?

4.   The brush hit the brass on the dresser.

5.   I like hot broth and fritters on cold winter days.

6.   Frank put the brass frame on the cross.

7.   The drone is a male bee.

8.   Why did Fred fill the drum to the brim?

9.   I hate crabs and frogs.

10. Mary will get a frock for her birthday.

gr   pr

gr Practise the consonants **g** and **r** separately before blending them.
Think of as many words as you can that begin with **gr** .

Then practise the builders.

gra	**gre**	**gro**	**gru**	**gri**
Box 1	Box 2	Box 3	Box 4	Box 5
grab	Gregory	grog	grub	grip
grand	gr**ee**n	grope	gruff	grin
grass	grenade	grove	grunt	grime

ee together make the long vowel sound $\bar{e}$.

pr Practise the consonants **p** and **r** separately before blending them.
Think of as many words as you can that begin with **pr** .

Then practise the builders

pra	**pre**	**pro**	**pru**	**pri**
Box 6	Box 7	Box 8	Box 9	Box 10
pram	press	prop	prune	prim
prank	present	problem	pruned	pride
practise	prefer	profit	pruning	prize

tr

tr	Practise the consonants **t** and **r** separately before blending them. Think of as many words as you can that begin with **tr** .

Then practise the builders.

tra	**tre**	**tro**	**tru**	**tri**
Box 1	Box 2	Box 3	Box 4	Box 5
trap track trash	trend trench tree	trot trotting trolley	truck trust trumpet	trip trick tribe

Things to remember

1. The **y** at the end of a word can sound like $\bar{e}$ or $\bar{i}$.
2. A short word ending in **e** gives **a, o, u, e,** or **i** its own name.
3. Two of the same consonants sound as one, tro**ll**ey, dre**ss**.
4. **ee** together make the long vowel sound $\bar{e}$ (its own name), tr**ee**, gr**ee**n.

bl   fl

 Practise the consonants **b** and **l** separately
before blending them.
Think of as many words as you can that
begin with **bl** .

Then practise the builders.

bla	**ble**	**blo**	**blu**	**bli**
Box 1	Box 2	Box 3	Box 4	Box 5
black blade blame	bled blend bless	blot blob blonde	blunt blush blunder	blink blister bliss

 Practise the consonants **f** and **l** separately
before blending them.
Think of as many words as you can that
begin with **fl** .

Then practise the builders

fla	**fle**	**flo**	**flu**	**fli**
Box 6	Box 7	Box 8	Box 9	Box 10
flap flag flash	fled flex flesh	flop flog flock	fluff flush fluke	flip flit flick

Practise the consonants **g** and **l** separately before blending them.
Think of as many words as you can that begin with **gl** .

Then practise the builders.

gla	**gle**	**glo**	**glu**	**gli**
Box 1	Box 2	Box 3	Box 4	Box 5
glad	glen	gloss	glum	glimmer
glass	glee	globe	glut	glitter
glade	gl**ea**m	glow	glutton	glide

gl**ea**m: In this word the **ea** has a long $\bar{e}$ sound.

 Practise the consonants **p** and **l** separately before blending them.
Think of as many words as you can that begin with **pl** .

Then practise the builders

pla	**ple**	**plo**	**plu**
Box 6	Box 7	Box 8	Box 9
plan	plenty	plod	plug
plant	pledge	plot	plum
plane	please	plop	plush

Time for a test

1. When I am away give the plants plenty of water.

2. Fluff the cat ran after the flock of blackbirds.

3. If you drop the globe my brother will blame me.

4. My mum makes plum cake and flap jacks every Saturday.

5. The blonde girl fled when she saw the brute.

6. The trolley will not glide on the grass.

7. Grab the frame and drop it in the truck.

8. The boy with the brass trumpet made a blunder.

9. The brush broke the glass in the shed at the cricket pitch.

10. I am glad I went on the trip in a plane.

sl   cl

sl Practise the consonants **s** and **l** separately before blending them.
Think of as many words as you can that begin with sl .

Then practise the builders.

sla	**sle**	**slo**	**slu**	**sli**
Box 1	Box 2	Box 3	Box 4	Box 5
slap slam slack	slender sl**ee**p sl**ee**t	slop slog slope	slum slug slush	slip slick slide

ee sound as ē

cl Practise the consonants **c** and **l** separately before blending them. (**cl** sounds as kl)
Think of as many words as you can that begin with cl .

Then practise the builders

cla	**cle**	**clo**	**clu**	**cli**
Box 6	Box 7	Box 8	Box 9	Box 10
clap clad class	clever clerk cleft	clop clock cloth	club cluck clump	clip click cliff

Time for a test

1. Frank fell off a cliff yesterday and broke his leg.

2. Do not clap even if he is the best in class.

3. Can you see the clock in the club house?

4. If you slam the door the glass will crack.

5. I heard the horse go clip, clop on the track.

6. My uncle did a clever trick on Friday.

7. There is a clump of trees near the cleft.

8. Do not slip and slide in the slush.

9. Mum put the black slack on the fire.

10. Catch the wet cloth with the black glove.

Useful words

Box 1
one
two
three
four

Box 2
five
six
seven
eight

Box 3
nine
ten
once
twice

Box 4
first
second
third
fourth

Box 5
fifth
sixth
hour
minute

Box 6
twenty
fifty
sixty
seventy

Box 7
cold
hot
sunny
dull

Box 8
snow
frost
ice
dry

Box 9
happy
young
old
funny

Box 10
asleep
awake
read
write

Useful words

Box 11	Box 12	Box 13	Box 14	Box 15
inside	toys	before	children	seaside
outside	dolls	after	people	beach
under	football	gave	men	bucket
over	game	brought	women	spade

Box 16	Box 17	Box 18	Box 19	Box 20
money	bought	yesterday	every	table
price	paid	night	very	chair
change	sold	lunch	never	eat
count	sweets	evening	again	drink

64

Puzzle page

The first and the last letter of each word is missing.
To make the word you must use one of the pairs of letters in heavy print.
Use a different pair each time. The first one is done for you.

T	R	I	C	K	
	L	O	C		
	L	O	P		
	L	A	S		
	R	A	N		
	H	I	C		
	R	I	Z		
	A	T	C		
	H	E	L		
	R	U	S		

S	**E**
G	**D**
P	**E**
C	**H**
T	**K**
S	**L**
C	**K**
B	**H**
W	**H**
G	**S**

Tongue twisters

See how quickly you can read them.

1. Shall Sam shine the shell on the ship by the shore for the sale?

2. Frank has freckles and Fred has fresh fat fritters.

3. The black blister bled when the blunt blade dropped.

4. Three thin thrushes sat on three thick thorns.

5. Did the driver dip the brush and drip a drop on the dresser?

6. Shut the shop and show Sam your shin in the shed.

7. Which witch whispered when the white whistle blew.

8. Pick a thick chick and check the ticket in the jacket.

9. Chip, chap, chop. Check the churn on the bench at the church.

Silly sentences

Change the beginning sounds (underlined) to make proper sentences.

1. Why <u>f</u>id Fred <u>d</u>ill the <u>b</u>rum to the <u>d</u>rim?

2. My <u>f</u>irt was <u>g</u>irty when I <u>sh</u>ell in the <u>d</u>arden.

3. I eat <u>ch</u>ish and <u>f</u>ips in the <u>sh</u>ip <u>ch</u>op.

4. Put the <u>b</u>ock in your <u>p</u>ack <u>l</u>ocket.

5. Frank fell off a <u>br</u>iff yesterday and <u>cl</u>oke his leg.

6. I like <u>c</u>ot <u>fr</u>oth and <u>br</u>itters on <u>h</u>old winter days.

Silly sentences

Here are some mixed up sentences. Can you put the endings (underlined) in the right places to make proper sentences?

1. Did the fat cat <u>get a job</u>?

2. Put the milk <u>in the bog</u>.

3. The dog bit Pat <u>on the log box</u>.

4. The man got a cod <u>in the ribs</u>.

5. How did Sam <u>eat the rat</u>?

6. Jim put the lid <u>on the leg</u>.

7. The boy hit Peg <u>on the rod</u>.

8. The big men dug <u>in the cup</u>.

9. Mum fed <u>the wet rug</u>.

10. Do not rub <u>the hens</u>.

Fun with phonics

Here are some silly words. Can you read them?

lep	shem	bont	blont
dop	frip	dolp	drosp
rog	drog	seft	shelp
gep	blof	welf	thest
sem	wheg	milp	whirt
min	brin	bint	crilp
rif	crad	dask	drash
das	slup	fash	shast
wug	truf	fulb	trunt
bup	grat	rusp	stulp

Why not try to invent your own "silly words"?

Make a list.

NOTES

NOTES